Table of content

Introduction

Appendix

Appendix one

**Article 50 of the treaty on European Union.
The process of withdrawing from the European
Union.**

Introduction

The people of Britain voted for a British exit, or Brexit, from the EU in a historic referendum on Thursday June 23. The outcome has prompted jubilant celebrations among Euro sceptics around Europe and sent shock waves through the global economy. After the result, the pound fell to its lowest level since 1985 and David Cameron resigned as Prime Minister of this country on Friday.

He said: "I will do everything I can as Prime Minister to steady the ship over the coming weeks and months. But I do not think it would be right for me to try to be the captain that steers our country to its next destination."

The Conservative 1922 Committee believes that his successor should take up office by September 2, at which point the UK would embark on its two-year political divorce from the EU.

The next step is for Britain to tell the EU that it wants to go by using Article 50 (appendix 1) of the EU rulebook for the first time in history.

Sequel to the result of the referendum a lot of question has been arising, in order to fully comprehend what the whole thing is all about. Some questions like,

"What is EU"

"What is BREXIT"

"What happens if we leave EU" has been widely asked. This article was actually written to clarify the readers on what the whole process actually meant and the implication therein.

1. Explanation of basic terms

1.1 What is EU

EU an acronym which stands for European union is a union with twenty eight European nations namely Austria, Belgium, Bulgaria, Croatia, the Republic of Cyprus, Czech Republic, Denmark, Estonia, Finland, France, Germany, Greece, Hungary, Ireland, Italy, Latvia, Lithuania, Luxembourg, Malta, the Netherlands, Poland, Portugal, Romania, Slovakia, Slovenia, Spain, Sweden and united kingdom. It is founded upon numerous treaties and has undergone expansions that have taken it from 6 member states to 28, a majority of the states in Europe. The European Union is set up with the aim of ending the frequent and bloody wars between neighbours, which culminated in the Second World War. As of 1950, the European Coal and Steel Community begins to unite European countries economically and politically in order to secure lasting peace. The six founding countries are Belgium, France, Germany, Italy, Luxembourg and the Netherlands. The 1950s are dominated by a cold war between east and west. Protests in Hungary against the Communist regime are put down by Soviet tanks in 1956. In 1957, the Treaty of Rome creates the

European Economic Community (EEC), or 'Common Market'.The 1960s is a good period for the economy, helped by the fact that EU countries stop charging custom duties when they trade with each other. They also agree joint control over food production, so that everybody now has enough to eat - and soon there is even surplus agricultural produce. May 1968 becomes famous for student riots in Paris, and many changes in society and behaviour become associated with the so-called '68 generation'. Denmark, Ireland and the United Kingdom join the European Union on 1 January 1973, raising the number of Member States to nine. The short, yet brutal, Arab-Israeli war of October 1973 results in an energy crisis and economic problems in Europe. The last right-wing dictatorships in Europe come to an end with the overthrow of the Salazar regime in Portugal in 1974 and the death of General Franco of Spain in 1975. The EU regional policy starts to transfer huge sums of money to create jobs and infrastructure in poorer areas. The European Parliament increases its influence in EU affairs and in 1979 all citizens can, for the first time, elect their members directly. The fight against pollution intensifies in the 1970s. The EU adopts laws to protect the environment, introducing the notion of 'the polluter pays' for the first time. With the collapse of communism across central and eastern Europe, Europeans become closer neighbours. In 1993 the Single Market is completed with the 'four freedoms' of: movement of goods, services, people and money. The 1990s is also the decade of two treaties: the 'Maastricht' Treaty on European Union in 1993 and the Treaty of Amsterdam in 1999. People are concerned about how to protect the environment and also how Europeans can act together when it comes to security and defence matters. In 1995 the EU gains three more new members: Austria, Finland and Sweden. A small village in Luxembourg gives its name to the 'Schengen' agreements that gradually allow people to travel without having their passports checked at the borders. Millions of young people study in other countries with EU support. Communication is made easier as more and more people start using mobile phones and the internet. The euro is now the new currency for many Europeans. During the decade more and more countries adopt the euro. 11 September 2001 becomes synonymous with the 'War on Terror' after hijacked airliners are flown into buildings in New York and Washington. EU countries begin to work much more closely together to fight crime. The political divisions between east and west Europe are finally declared healed when no fewer than 10 new countries join the EU in 2004, followed by Bulgaria and Romania in 2007. A financial crisis hits the global economy in September 2008. The Treaty of Lisbon is ratified by all EU countries before entering into force in 2009. It provides the EU with modern institutions and more efficient working methods. The global economic crisis strikes hard in Europe. The EU helps several countries to confront their difficulties and establishes the 'Banking Union' to ensure safer and more reliable banks. In 2012, the European Union is awarded the Nobel Peace Prize. Croatia becomes the 28th member of the EU in 2013. Climate change is still high on the agenda and leaders agree to reduce harmful emissions. European elections are held in 2014 and more Eurosceptics are elected into the European Parliament. A new security policy is established in the wake of the annexation of Crimea by Russia. Religious extremism increases in the Middle East and various countries and regions around the world, leading to unrest and wars which result in many people fleeing their homes and seeking refuge in Europe. The EU is not only faced with the dilemma of how to take care of them, but also finds itself the target of several terrorist attacks. Apart from the ideas of federation, confederation, or customs union, the original development of the European Union was based on a supranational foundation that would "make war unthinkable and materially impossible" and reinforce democracy amongst its members as laid out by Robert Schuman and other leaders in the Schuman Declaration (1950) and the Europe Declaration (1951). This principle was at the heart of the European Coal and Steel Community (ECSC) (1951), the Treaty of Paris (1951), and later the Treaty of Rome (1958) which established the European Economic Community (EEC) and the European Atomic Energy Community (EAEC). Both the ECSC and EEC were later incorporated into the European Union while the EAEC maintains a distinct legal identity despite sharing members and institutions. The Maastricht Treaty (1992) created the European Union with its pillars system, including foreign and home affairs alongside the European Community. This in turn led to the creation of the single European currency, the euro (launched 1999). The Maastricht Treaty has been amended by the treaties of Amsterdam (1997), Nice (2001) and Lisbon (2007).

1.2 What is BREXIT

British withdrawal from the European Union, also shortened from "British exit" to Brexit, is a political goal that has been pursued by various individuals, advocacy groups, and political parties since the United Kingdom joined the precursor of the European Union (EU) in 1973. Withdrawal from the European Union has been a right of EU member states since 2007 under Article 50 of the Treaty on European Union.

In 1975, a referendum was held on the country's membership of the European Economic Community (EEC), later known as the EU. The outcome of the vote was approximately 67% in favour of the UK's continued membership of the EEC.

The UK electorate again addressed the question on 23 June 2016, in a referendum on the country's membership. This referendum was arranged by Parliament when it passed the European Union Referendum Act 2015. The result was 51.9% in support of an exit (17,410,742 votes) and 48.1% (16,141,241 votes) to remain with a turnout of 72.2% and 26,033 rejected ballots.

The exact process for the UK's withdrawal is uncertain under EU law, although it is generally expected to take longer than two years. Article 50 which governs the withdrawal has never been used before. The British Prime Minister David Cameron announced he will resign by October, while the First Minister of Scotland Nicola Sturgeon has said that Scotland may refuse legislative consent to dropping EU law in Scotland. The UK was not a signatory to the Treaty of Rome which created the EEC in 1957. The country subsequently applied to join the organisation in 1963 and again in 1967, but both applications were vetoed by the then President of France, Charles de Gaulle, ostensibly because "a number of aspects of Britain's economy, from working practices to agriculture" [had] "made Britain incompatible with Europe" and that Britain harboured a "deep-seated hostility" to any pan-European project.

Once de Gaulle had relinquished the French presidency, the UK made a third application for membership, which was successful. On 1 January 1973 the United Kingdom joined the EEC, then often referred to in the UK as the "Common Market". This was done under the Conservative

Prime Minister Edward Heath. The opposition Labour Party, led by Harold Wilson, contested the October 1974 general election with a commitment to renegotiate Britain's terms of membership of the EEC and then hold a referendum on whether to remain in the EEC on the new terms. In 2012, Prime Minister David Cameron rejected calls for a referendum on the UK's EU membership, but suggested the possibility of a future referendum to gauge public support. According to the BBC, "The prime minister acknowledged the need to ensure the UK's position within the European Union had 'the full-hearted support of the British people' but they needed to show 'tactical and strategic patience'. "In January 2013, Cameron announced that a Conservative government would hold an in-out referendum on EU membership before the end of 2017, on a renegotiated package, if elected in 2015. The Conservative Party won the 2015 general election with a majority. Soon afterwards the European Union Referendum Act 2015 was introduced into Parliament to enable the referendum. Despite being in favour of remaining in a reformed European Union himself, Cameron announced that Conservative Ministers and MPs were free to campaign in favour of remaining in the EU or leaving it, according to their conscience. This decision came after mounting pressure for a free vote for ministers. In an exception to the usual rule of cabinet collective responsibility, Cameron allowed cabinet ministers to publicly campaign for EU withdrawal.

In a speech to the House of Commons on 22 February 2016, Cameron announced a referendum date of 23 June 2016 and set out the legal framework for withdrawal from the European Union in circumstances where there was a referendum majority vote to leave, citing Article 50 of the Lisbon Treaty. Cameron spoke of an intention to trigger the Article 50 process immediately following a leave vote and of the "two-year time period to negotiate the arrangements for exit." The official campaign group for leaving the EU was Vote Leave. Other major campaign groups included Leave.EU, Grass roots Out, and Better Off Out, while non-EU affiliated organisations also campaigned for the United Kingdom's withdrawal, such as the Commonwealth Freedom of Movement Organisation. The official campaign to stay in the EU, chaired by Stuart Rose, was known as Britain Stronger in Europe, or informally as Remain.

Other campaigns supporting remaining in the EU included Conservatives In, Labour in for Britain, #INtogether (Liberal Democrats), Greens for a Better Europe, Scientists for EU, Environmentalists For Europe, Universities for Europe and Another Europe is Possible. Public opinion on whether the UK should leave the EU or stay has varied. An October 2015 analysis of polling suggested that younger voters tend to support remaining in the EU, whereas older voters tend to support leaving, but there is no gender split in attitudes. Article 50 of the Treaty on European Union provides that: "Any Member State may decide to withdraw from the Union in accordance with its own constitutional requirements." Article 50 was inserted by the Lisbon Treaty in 2007, before which the treaties were silent on the possibility of withdrawal from the European Union. Once a member state has notified the European Council of its intent to leave the EU, a period begins during which a leaving agreement is negotiated setting out the arrangements for the withdrawal and outlining the country's future relationship with the Union. For the agreement to enter into force it needs to be approved by at least 72 percent of the continuing member states representing at least 65 percent of their population, and the consent of the European Parliament. The treaties cease to apply to the member state concerned on the entry into force of the leaving agreement, or in the absence of such an agreement, two years after the member state notified the European Council of its intent to leave, although this period can be extended by unanimous agreement of the European Council. Article 50 termination notice starts a two year period, known as a Sunset Period, when the details of a Withdrawal Agreement are negotiated. If the Sunset Period is not extended beyond the two year period or ratified by unanimous agreement of all Member EU States and if no Withdrawal Agreement is entered into within such two year period, then the UK will automatically cease to be a Member State of the EU after two years. Instead of going through the internal EU process, the UK could also unilaterally withdraw by repealing the enabling European Communities Act 1972 (UK). As was the case with the Scottish independence referendum two years earlier, the 2016 referendum did not directly require the government to do anything in particular. It does not require the government to initiate, or even schedule, the Article 50 procedure, although David Cameron stated during the campaign that he would invoke Article 50 straight away in the event of a leave victory. Some[who?] have suggested that a second referendum could be held to "confirm" the decision to leave following negotiations. However, there is no established, formal process for doing so. Alan Renwick of the Constitution Unit of University College London argues that Article 50 negotiations cannot be used to renegotiate the conditions of future membership and that Article 50 does not provide the legal basis of withdrawing a decision to leave. The UK government has stated that they would expect a leave vote to be followed by withdrawal, not by a second vote. EU politicians [who?] largely agree. Following the referendum result, Cameron announced that he would resign before the Conservative party conference in October, and that it would be for the incoming Prime Minister to invoke Article 50 of the EU Treaty.

However, a petition to the UK Parliament for a second referendum reached over 3.3 million signatures within four days. It asked: "We the under signed call upon HM Government to implement a rule that if the remain or leave vote is less than 60% based a turnout less than 75%

there should be another referendum." The referendum of 23 June fulfils these conditions. Having received more than 100,000 signatures, the petition must receive a government response and be considered for a parliamentary debate.

2 The relationship between Britain and EU

On January 1st 1973 Britain finally joined the EU after their first attempt to join the Common Market was vetoed by Charles de Gaulle, who was said to be worried about English taking over as Europe's main language. Britain was finally allowed into European Economic Community under Conservative Prime Minister Edward Heath, but within a year the nation called for major changes to the Common Agricultural Policy, "fairer methods of financing the budget" and solutions to monetary problems. There are 73 members of the European Parliament from the UK. The Council of the EU, national ministers meet regularly to adopt EU laws and coordinate policies. Council meetings are regularly attended by representatives from the UK government, depending on the policy area being addressed. The Council of the EU doesn't have a permanent, single-person president (like e.g. the Commission or Parliament). Instead, its work is led by the country holding the Council presidency, which rotates every 6 months.

During these 6 months, ministers from that country's government chair and help determine the agenda of Council meetings in each policy area, and facilitate dialogue with the other EU institutions.

Dates of UK presidencies:

Jan-Jun 1977 | Jul-Dec 1981 | Jul-Dec 1992 | Jan-Jun 1998 | Jul-Dec 2005.

The Commissioner nominated by the UK to the European Commission is Jonathan Hill, who is responsible for Financial Stability, Financial Services and Capital Markets Union.

The Commission is represented in each EU country by a local office, called a "representation".

Commission representation in the United Kingdom

The United Kingdom has 25 representatives on the European Economic and Social Committee. This advisory body – representing employers, workers and other interest groups – is consulted on proposed laws, to get a better idea of the possible changes to work and social situations in member countries.

The United Kingdom has 24 representatives on the Committee of the Regions, the EU's assembly of regional and local representatives. This advisory body is consulted on proposed laws, to ensure these laws take account of the perspective from each region of the EU.

The UK also communicates with the EU institutions through its permanent representation in Brussels. As the United Kingdom's "embassy to the EU", its main task is to ensure that the country's interests and policies are pursued as effectively as possible in the EU.

Member countries' financial contributions to the EU budget are shared fairly, according to means. The larger your country's economy, the more it pays – and vice versa. The EU budget doesn't aim to redistribute wealth, but rather to focus on the needs of all Europeans as a whole.

Breakdown of the UK's finances with the EU in 2014:

Total EU spending in the UK: € 6.985 billion

Total EU spending as % of the UK's gross national income (GNI): 0.32 %

Total UK contribution to the EU budget: € 11.342 billion

The UK's Contribution to the EU budget as % of its GNI: 0.52 %

The money paid into the EU budget by the UK helps fund programmes and projects in all EU countries - like building roads, subsidising researchers and protecting the environment.

3 The reasons behind BREXIT

The assertion that leaving the EU would free up £350m a week extra to spend on the NHS is the kind of political slogan that campaigns dream of: striking, easy to understand and attractive to voters of different ages and political persuasion.

No surprise then that Vote Leave chose to splash it across the side of their battle bus.

The fact that the claim does not stand up to much scrutiny - the figure is calculated using sums which were disputed by the Treasury Select Committee and described as potentially misleading by the UK Statistics Authority - did not reduce its potency.

Remain campaigner Angela Eagle may have told her opponents to "get that lie off your bus" but polling suggests it gained traction and was the single most remembered figure from the campaign, with many people believing that money handed over to the EU to be a member should be spent in the UK instead.

In that sense, it served as a powerful illustration of how the UK could be Britons who want to exit the European Union see exactly that unfolding, as they work to undo the U.K.'s 1973 move to join the EU. Meanwhile, Brexit's opponents argue it's this week that the nation is hurtling toward a big mistake that will set back an entire generation.

While the public debate has focused on economic arguments — such as whether an exit would shrink or boost the U.K. economy — experienced pundits suggest voters will be driven by emotions, deciding with their hearts, not their heads.better off outside the EU. Britons who want to exit the European Union see exactly that unfolding, as they work to undo the U.K.'s 1973 move to join the EU. Meanwhile, Brexit's opponents argue it's this week that the nation is hurtling toward a big mistake that will set back an entire generation.

While the public debate has focused on economic arguments — such as whether an exit would shrink or boost the U.K. economy — experienced pundits suggest voters will be driven by emotions,

Immigration, a touchy subject in the U.S., is important to U.K. voters, especially given Europe's migrant crisis.

The leave campaigns "trump card" is "immigration and strong borders, the issue that has remained at or near the top of voters' concerns for years," said Clare Foges, a former speech writer for U.K. Prime

Minister David Cameron, in a column for The Times of London.

The EU has struggled to address the migrant crisis effectively, and Brexiteers argue the U.K. needs to avoid getting dragged down by the blocs actions or lack thereof. Migrants are taking jobs and places in schools from British citizens, "outers" argue. "The EU response to the migration crisis is a Five Nations free-for-all with an invitation to Macedonia, Montenegro, Serbia, Albania and Turkey to join the Union," said Michael Gove, a Brexit supporter and the U.K.'s justice secretary, in a column. "Because we cannot control our borders, public services such as the NHS will face an unquantifiable strain as millions more become EU citizens and have the right to move to the U.K."

Britain's economy would be better off after an exit, according to London mayor Boris Johnson, arguably the most prominent politician in the leave camp. He has likened it to an escape from prison.

The U.K. would be more competitive because it could make its own trade deals with other nations and legislate in the interest of British manufacturing, Johnson argued in March.

The billionaire co-founder of broker Hargreaves Landsdowne has argued a Brexit "would be the biggest stimulus to get our butts in gear," likening it to the Dunkirk retreat during World War II.

Such appeals to national pride and even nostalgia have big roles in the Brexit pitches.

"I yearn for the days when my (gorgeous navy blue) passport got stamped when I went anywhere in Europe," said English actress and Brexit supporter Liz Hurley in a column for a magazine. U.K. passports are now burgundy and conform to an EU format.

The EU "has become centralising, regulating and controlling, the opposite of what is needed for jobs and future success," said Gerard Lyons, a leave supporter and Johnson's chief economic adviser, in a column for The London Evening Standard.

Countries that succeed in the future global economy will "need to be flexible, adaptable and control their own destiny. Brexit allows us this," he said.

Brexit backers complain about rules set in Brussels that stipulate such things as the curvature of cucumbers and bananas — and that even override Britain's own laws.

The EU is a "customs area" that aims to protect the agricultural and manufacturing industries, said Lyons in his column. It does this by setting quotas, giving handouts to farmers and putting restrictions on just where fishing boats can trawl, the argument goes.

That "results in people across the EU paying more for the prices of these things compared with world markets. With Brexit, people would suddenly face cheaper prices for food, as we would be paying world prices," Lyons argued

4 The consequences of brexit

Voters have voted in favor of Brexit: British exit from the European Union. That means that in the coming months, British and European leaders will begin negotiating the terms of Britain's departure. Britain's exit will affect the British economy, immigration policy, and lots more. It will take years for the full consequences to become clear. But here are some of the most important changes we can expect in the coming months.

4.1. Economic consequences

Britain's financial and professional services industry – banks, accountants, corporate lawyers, investment managers is a significant contributor to GDP (around 12%, which is more than manufacturing), a senior figure at the European Central Bank said banks in the City of London risked being stripped of their lucrative EU "passports" that allow them to sell services to the rest of the union. The City, as the industry is better known, will want to retain that passport; otherwise it will not, for instance, be able to advise on a mega-euro takeover in Germany or sell euro-denominated products such as derivatives. To do that simply, the City will need to join the single market, or the European Economic Area that encapsulates the EU and non-members such as Norway. That will, in turn, require accepting freedom of movement. Or the City can go it alone and operate in a much looser regulatory environment, which will please hedge funds and bankers keen to avoid an EU-imposed cap on bonus payments. Official trade statistics show that the European Union is the destination for about half of all British goods exports. The trading links are bigger if we include the countries that the United Kingdom trades freely with because they have a free trade agreement with the European Union. These agreements mean that 63% of Britain's goods exports are linked to European Union membership.

Financial services have more to lose immediately after a European Union exit than most other sectors of the economy. Even in the best case, in which passporting rights were preserved, the United Kingdom would still lose influence over the single market's rules. The City would probably be hurt in the short term, but it would not spell disaster. The City's competitive advantage is founded on more than just unfettered access to the single market. A European Union exit would enable the United Kingdom to broker trade deals with emerging markets that could pay dividends for the financial services sector in the long run.

It is highly probable that a favourable trade agreement would be reached after Brexit as there are advantages for both sides in continuing a close commercial arrangement. But the worst-case scenario, in which Britain faces tariffs under 'most-favoured nation' rules, is certainly no disaster. Exporters would face some additional costs, such as complying with the European Union's rules of origin, if they were outside the single market. However, these factors would be an inconvenience rather than a major barrier to trade. In addition, fears that exporters would be left high and dry the day after the Brexit vote are unfounded. Under the Lisbon Treaty, a country leaving the European Union has 2 years in which to negotiate a withdrawal agreement. In addition, falling tariffs, the decline in manufacturing and Europe's diminishing importance in the global economy mean we doubt that even the absence of a trade deal with the European Union would hurt the United Kingdom's overall exports materially. The benefits of being in the European Union are smaller than they were a few decades ago, when a Brexit would have been a far bigger deal. However, the effects will vary across sectors. Brexit would give Britain a crucial opportunity by allowing it to broker its own trade deals with non-European Union countries; indeed Britain could even have a unilateral free trade policy. Non-European Union countries may find negotiating with Britain easier and quicker than dealing with the European Union's bureaucratic machine, as Switzerland has shown.

The production sectors in the economy face a more uncertain outcome than services. The range of potential outcomes is more variable as production sectors are more dependent on whether or not the United Kingdom agrees a trading agreement with the European Union and the nature of any such agreement. The possibility of tariffs on goods exports to the European Union gives greater downside potential, while the opportunity to open up trade with other countries or to increase the sector's competitiveness through greater competition or cheaper inputs gives it more upside potential. In the short run, uncertainty about Britain's future relationship with the EU, its largest trading partner, could push the UK into a recession. The British pound has lost about 9 percent of its value since June 23 vote, and Britain's FTSE 100 stock index lost 3 percent of its value in Friday trading. When you consider that the FTSE is priced in pounds that means British stocks are down more than 10 percent in real terms. And that volatility reflects market worries about more severe consequences in the months ahead. With Cameron out of power, Britain's prospects of negotiating a favourable deal with the EU could be weakened. The EU may decide to strike a hard bargain to discourage other countries from leaving the EU. Or the UK's new leader might not be willing to accept the kind of restrictions that come with a Norway-style deal. And that could create serious problems for businesses based in the UK. Critics say the economic effects could be large. The UK government has estimated that exiting the EU could cause the British economy to be between 3.8 and 7.5 percent smaller by 2030 — depending on how well negotiations for access to the European market ultimately go. Other reports have found smaller but still significant impacts.

4.2 Immigration impacts of Brexit

Annual net migration from Europe has more than doubled since 2012, reaching 183,000 in March

2015. Immigration from the European Union is currently boosting the workforce by around 0.5% a year. This has helped support the economy's ability to grow without pushing up wage growth and inflation, keeping interest rates lower for longer. Whether the United Kingdom gains any powers to restrict immigration from Europe will depend on its future relationship with the European Union. If Britain wanted to retain full access to the single market, it may have to keep the free movement of labour between the United Kingdom and the Union. But this is unlikely. Policy is far more likely to change to restrict the number of low skilled workers entering the country and shift towards attracting more highly skilled workers. This would be a potential headache for low-wage sectors heavily dependent on migrant labour, such as agriculture, but could benefit other sectors with a shortage of highly skilled labour. Overall, policy would shift to be more specifically designed for Britain's migration requirements.

One of the most important and controversial achievements of the EU was the establishment of the principle of free movement among EU countries. A citizen of one EU country has an unfettered right to live and work anywhere in the EU. Both Britons and foreigners have taken advantage of this opportunity. Currently there are about 1.2 million Brits living in other EU countries, while about 3 million non-British EU nationals live in Britain. Thanks to EU rules, they were able to move across the English Channel with a minimum of paperwork. Britain's exit from the EU could change that profoundly. It's possible, of course, that Britain could negotiate a new treaty with the EU that continues to allow free movement between the UK and the EU. But resentment of EU immigrants — especially from poorer, economically struggling countries like Poland and Lithuania — was a key force driving support for Brexit. So the British government will be under immense pressure to refuse to continue the current arrangement. At a minimum, that would mean that people moving to or from Britain would need to worry about passports and residency rules. And it could mean that some British immigrants may lose their right to continue living and working in the UK and be deported.

4.3 Security and foreign policy impacts of Brexit

Britain's decision to leave the European Union could make it more difficult to maintain transatlantic agreement on sanctions on Russia over Ukraine, and distract Britain and the E.U. from other pressing foreign policy issues as they disentangle their ties, On the day after the historic vote known as Brexit, with financial markets plummeting worldwide, foreign policy and national security analysts were trying to predict the implications for the United States in its relations with the E.U and Britain, allies that separately and together have been key partners on a host of global issues, from the war in Syria to the nuclear deal with Iran.

Some adversaries immediately saw chinks in Europe's armor as a result of the vote. Politicians in Moscow predicted it would sap the E.U. of a strong member and ultimately hasten the lifting of sanctions with damaging effects for the United States the most important long-term consequence of all this is that the exit will take Europe away from the anglo-saxons, meaning from the USA," said the Kremlin's small-business ombudsman, Boris Titov, in a Facebook post. "It's not the independence of Britain from Europe, but the independence of Europe from the USA." Michael McFaul, a former U.S. ambassador to Russia, tweeted as much, writing that Russian President

Vladi-mir "Putin benefits from a weaker Europe. UK vote makes EU weaker. It's just that simple."

But analysts said the British vote could signal a more inward-looking Europe as it copes with the decision.

"One of the strongest cards we have to play against Putin is transatlantic unity," said Julianne Smith, a national security analyst with the Centre for a New American Security. "This creates two years of navel gazing and internal debate about where we go from here and Britain's place in Europe. We lose our ability to stand together." The loss of a British voice within the E.U. means Washington will have one less like-minded friend in diplomatic issues involving Europeans. "It's still an important partner, one of the most militarily capable and diplomatically accomplished partners there is," said Karen Donfried, president of the German Marshall Fund of the United States. "To not have the E.U. benefit from the role Britain plays is a net negative." But some analysts say the concerns are being overblown. Britain's military will continue to operate within NATO, which is separate from the E.U.

Britain is providing troops and equipment to coalitions that are waging military operations in

Iraq, Yemen and Syria. Michael O'Hanlon, a national security analyst with the Brookings Institution, said that while Britain's contribution is larger than its size would warrant, it is still no more than 10 to 15 percent of what the United States commits. The stakes are important, but they're not astronomically big to begin with," he said. "It may have repercussions down the road," he said of Britain's breakup from the E.U. "Maybe its military will become a little smaller. But we need to take a chill pill on worries about the downsides of withdrawal." Indeed, some argue that Britain's exit from the E.U. could free London to act more forcefully and, for instance, impose harsher sanctions against Russia.

"A sovereign Britain, one able to act completely independently of the supranational European Union, will be a more powerful force on the international stage than it is now," said Nile Gardiner, a onetime aide to former Prime Minister Margaret Thatcher who now heads the Heritage Foundation's Center for Freedom that is named after her. "I think that far from welcoming Brexit, Putin fears it." The biggest unknown is whether the British move will have a cascading effect. "If three or four other countries do this as a copycat, then we have a more interesting problem," said Barry Pavel, director of the Atlantic Council's Brent Scowcroft Centre on International Security. "They're opting out of an economic union, and I don't think it's good, but it's not as catastrophic as people are playing out yet. We have to wait and see what happens."

Anti-E.U. parties in several European countries have said they plan to agitate for a referendum as Britain did. Marian L. Tupy, who analyses the effects of globalization at the Cato Institutes Centre on Global Liberty and Prosperity, called the British vote "the beginning of the end for the European Union." With every electoral cycle, pro-European parties are losing support and parties the E.U. calls dismissively 'populist' are increasing in popularity," he said. "It was only a matter of time before an E.U. country had either elected an anti-European government or held a referendum on it. The British were the first." Tupy, who supports the breakaway as an expression of freedom, considers the security aspects negligible. The United States shares its intelligence more judiciously with other countries on the European continent than it does with Britain, Smith of the Center for a New American Security said intelligence sharing and cooperation inevitably will be weakened in a divided Europe. "Whether it's counter terrorism or a resurgent Russia or challenges in the Middle East, our ability to put forward common strategies is in question in a very distressed Europe," she said. "This is a crushing blow."

APPENDIX ONE

Article 50 of the treaty on European Union. The process of withdrawing from the European Union.

Article 50 of the Treaty on European Union provides as follows:

"1. Any Member State may decide to withdraw from the Union in accordance with its own constitutional requirements.

"2. A Member State which decides to withdraw shall notify the European Council of its intention. In the light of the guidelines provided by the European Council, the Union shall negotiate and conclude an agreement with that State, setting out the arrangements for its withdrawal, taking account of the framework for its future relationship with the Union. That agreement shall be negotiated in accordance with Article 218(3) of the Treaty on the Functioning of the European Union. It shall be concluded on behalf of the Union by the Council, acting by a qualified majority, after obtaining the consent of the European Parliament.

"3. The Treaties shall cease to apply to the State in question from the date of entry into force of the withdrawal agreement or, failing that, two years after the notification referred to in paragraph 2, unless the European Council, in agreement with the Member State concerned, unanimously decides to extend this period.

"4. For the purposes of paragraphs 2 and 3, the member of the European Council or of the Council representing the withdrawing Member State shall not participate in the discussions of the European Council or Council or in decisions concerning it. A qualified majority shall be defined in accordance with Article 238(3)(b) of the Treaty on the Functioning of the European Union.

"5. If a State which has withdrawn from the Union asks to rejoin, its request shall be subject to the procedure referred to in Article 49

www.ingramcontent.com/pod-product-compliance
Lightning Source LLC
Chambersburg PA
CBHW070844310526
45793CB00011B/534